# LM SR STEAM

## 1923 - 1948

H. C. CASSERLEY

D. BRADFORD BARTON LIMITED

**Frontispiece:** a north-bound freight on the old Highland Railway crossing the viaduct at 'Soldier's Leap' over the River Garry through the famous Pass of Killiecrankie, July 1931. The engine is No. 13104 (later 2804), one of the Horwich design of mixed traffic 2-6-0s, a type introduced to the Highland in 1929, and which did good work on that difficult line before being displaced by the ubiquitous Stanier 'Black Fives' in 1934.

© copyright D. Bradford Barton Ltd 1975 □ ISBN 0 85153 257 8 □ Set in Monotype Bembo and printed by offset litho by H. E. Warne Ltd, of London and St. Austell, for the publishers D. Bradford Barton Ltd, of Trethellan House, Truro, Cornwall

*No. 5902, Sir Frank Ree (later renumbered and renamed 5501 St. Dunstans), one of the original 'Patriot' Class introduced by Sir Henry Fowler in 1930, was nominally a rebuild of a LNWR 'Claughton', but was in fact virtually a completely new engine of quite different design. It is seen here with a Liverpool to Birmingham express near Penkridge.*
*[W. Leslie Good]*

# introduction

The London Midland & Scottish Railway came into being on 1 January 1923 as a result of the Railways Act of 1921, under which Government decree all of the hundred or so independent railways then existing were, with a few minor exceptions, compulsorily amalgamated into four groups. The LMS was by far the largest of the resulting new entities, the others being the London & North Eastern, the Great Western—in this case it was, in effect, one large company absorbing a number of other lesser ones and retaining its old title—and the Southern.

The principal constituents of the newly formed LMS were the combined London & North Western and Lancashire & Yorkshire, which had themselves amalgamated a year earlier on 1 January 1922—although with little or no outward evidence of any change—the Midland (third largest of the pre-Grouping railways), three of the Scottish railways, the Caledonian, Glasgow & South Western, and Highland, together with a number of smaller lines. Amongst the latter may be mentioned the North Stafford, Furness, Maryport & Carlisle, Wirral, Stratford-on-Avon & Midland Junction, plus a few other minor concerns.

The LMS also became part-owners of three of the country's largest joint lines, the Somerset & Dorset in conjunction with the Southern, the Midland and Great Northern Joint, of which the other partner was the London and North Eastern, and the Cheshire Lines, also joint with the LNER. The latter was in practice almost entirely responsible for the working of the CLC, providing the locomotives, although the Committee possessed its own rolling stock. The S&DJR and M&GNJR each had its own locomotives and stock, and for several years maintained its individual workshops, although these were eventually closed, the S&DJR locomotives being merged into the LMS. The M&GNJR was taken over by the LNER, which as a consequence does not come into the present volume.

As if this were not enough, however, the LMS also inherited ownership of the old Belfast & Northern Counties Railway in Ireland, which had been absorbed by the Midland in 1903. Since that date it had been known as the Northern Counties Committee of the MR, and under the new regime it now became the LMS-NCC. The ever-enterprising Midland had even acquired a part interest in the 3′ gauge County Donegal Railway in the north-west of Ireland, under a curious joint ownership with the Great Northern Railway of Ireland, and this too passed on to the LMS. Both of these Irish interests were to last until the end of the Grouping era in 1948.

This whole wide-embracing network had the result that the engines and trains of the LMS could regularly be seen over a very wide area of Great Britain, ranging from Thurso in the far north to Bournemouth in the south, and from Shoeburyness, Cambridge, Peterborough, Lincoln and Goole in the east (and even on less regular occasions to Yarmouth and Lowestoft) to Holyhead and Swansea in the west. The following selection of photographs endeavours to portray typical engine and train views to be seen during that period.

The second Stanier Pacific, No. 6201 *Princess Elizabeth*, leaving Northchurch tunnel near Berkhamsted, on a down Liverpool express, August 1939. Happily, this engine is now preserved.

A view of another of the class, No. 6203 *Princess Margaret Rose*, on an up Scottish express near Gretna, May 1936. This engine, too, is luckily still in existence; for many years it was on exhibition at Butlin's Holiday Camp, Pwllheli, but has recently been acquired by the Midland Railway Company Preservation Society.

Sir William Stanier came to the LMS from the Great Western in 1932, and proceeded to revolutionise the locomotive stock by the introduction of much larger express engines than had hitherto been in use. His first venture was, however, less spectacular, consisting of a series of ten 0-4-4Ts for pull-and-push working. No. 6408 (later 1908) is seen here at Watford Junction in February 1936 on the St. Albans branch train.

In 1937 came the 'Coronation' Class, an improved version of Stanier's Pacifics, with a startling form of streamlining for working the newly introduced 'Coronation Scot', the 401½ miles between Euston and Glasgow being covered in 6½ hours, the fastest so far scheduled for regular operation, and in direct competition with the LNER's 'Coronation' between King's Cross and Edinburgh. Apart from the streamlining, a new livery was introduced, consisting of blue—very much akin to the present all-pervading BR colour—with white horizontal lining applied to both engine and coaches. The up train is seen here in August 1939 behind No. 6222 *Queen Mary*, having passed Tring and accelerating to a final burst of speed for the last thirty miles to Euston.

Some of the 'Coronation'—or 'Duchess' Class as the later ones were called—were built without streamlining, and all eventually had this feature removed. No. 6246 *City of Manchester* is seen here in May 1947 calling at Crewe on a north-bound express.

The third of the original Pacifics to be built, No. 6202, was an entirely experimental engine, with turbine propulsion in place of conventional cylinders and valve gear. It ran successfully for several years in this form, almost entirely on a regular schedule on the 8.30 a.m. Euston to Liverpool and 5.25 p.m. return, and is seen here entering Watford in early 1948. Eventually rebuilt on orthodox lines, No. 6202 had a tragically short career in this form, being damaged beyond repair in the Harrow disaster of October 1952.

Another view of one of the later Pacifics built without the streamlining casing, No. 6251 *City of Nottingham*. Photographed at Polmadie in 1945 soon after construction, it has not yet received the smoke deflectors alongside the smokebox, which were found to be necessary on some classes to avoid steam drifting back and obscuring the driver's view. With it is a former Caledonian 4-6-0, No. 14630.

Sir William Stanier's new 'Jubilee' Class was a design built for general main line express passenger trains on all but the heaviest top link duties and did remarkably good work right to the end of steam, particularly on the Midland division. First engine of the class, No. 5552 *Silver Jubilee*, is seen passing Longbridge Junction, near Birmingham, on a Bristol express in May 1935, in an experimental livery of plain black with polished chromium lettering, boiler bands, and dome.

'Patriot' No. 5532 *Illustrious* on arrival at Euston, December 1938, with an express from Blackpool.

The great freeze of March 1947: No. 5666 *Cornwallis* heading through Berkhamsted with an up overnight sleeping-car train, several hours late with obvious indication of having encountered, apparently successfully, severe snowdrifts.

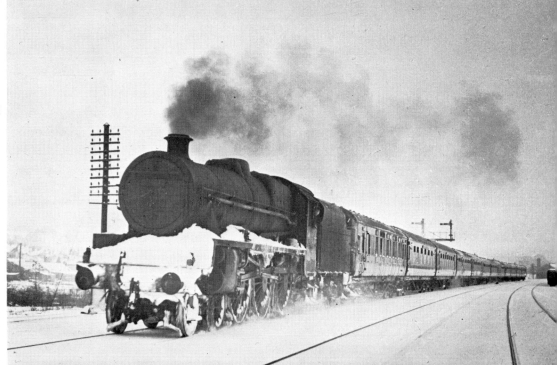

Another early view of a 'Jubilee', this time in normal LMS maroon livery—
No. 5583 *Assam*, near Gretna in May 1936 on a north-bound express.

'Jubilee' No. 5736 *Phoenix*, in original condition, passing Bourne End crossing with an up express in August 1939. This was the scene of a disastrous accident in October 1945, when a train took the crossing at full speed, for reasons never satisfactorily explained, instead of the normal reduction to 15 mph, and plunged into the embankment below (see also page 18). No. 5736, together with No. 5735 *Comet*, was later rebuilt with larger boiler into Class 6P, but these were the only 'Jubilees' to be so treated.

Another memory of the March 1947 freeze - two views of rebuilt 'Patriot' No. 5526 *Morecambe and Heysham* with a down express north of Northchurch Tunnel. As with many other modern designs, it was eventually found necessary to fit smokebox deflectors to avoid the nuisance and danger of drifting steam obscuring the view from the footplate.

Rebuilt 'Royal Scot'
No. 6116 *Irish Guardsman*
on an up express leaving
Northchurch Tunnel,
May 1948.

No. 46149 *The Middlesex
Regiment*, at the same
location, and
photographed on the
same day as the above
illustration, has already
received its BR number,
but is still in LMS livery.
At that time, for express
engines, this was black,
with maroon outlined in
straw-coloured lining on
the framing and cab
edging, giving just a
faint reminiscence of the
old crimson lake,
inherited originally from
the Midland of pre-war
years, and revived to a
very limited extent by
BR on a few Pacifics in
the 1960s.

One of the well known Stanier 'Black Fives'—undoubtedly amongst the most successful general purpose designs ever to be seen in this country. No less than 842 of them were built. No. 5280, seen here passing Wellingborough, is on a down Midland line express, July 1937.

The aftermath of the Bourne End accident of 1945 already referred to on page 15. After several weeks lying at the bottom of the embankment, No. 6157 *The Royal Artilleryman* was finally retrieved and re-railed on 28 October, and is seen here being prepared for towing away for repair and rebuilding.

Another 'Black Five', No. 5440, this time on a stopping train on the Somerset & Dorset Joint Railway near Stalbridge, July 1938.

Fowler 2-6-2T No. 16 running into Clapham station, in West Yorkshire, on a local off the Ingleton branch (now entirely closed).

Another Fowler 2-6-2T, No. 15520 (later No. 21), near Elstree on a local from St. Pancras to Luton. This was one of a batch which were fitted with condensing apparatus for working through the tunnels to Moorgate over the 'widened' lines of the Metropolitan Railway.

A typical suburban train on the old LNWR line from Euston to Tring and Bletchley, near Berkhamsted, March 1948, with Fowler 2-6-4T No. 2304.

Sir Henry Fowler's successor, Sir William Stanier, continued to build these very successful 2-6-4Ts with his own modifications, chief of which was the provision of a taper boiler. This is one of a batch built with three cylinders instead of two, specially for working on the Tilbury section; No. 2532 on an up Southend train passing Plaistow, June 1945.

Fowler 2-6-4T No. 2344, with an up Tring to Euston local, March 1947. Drifting snow has already partly covered the rails since the passage of the previous train.

One of the Horwich design of 2-6-0s introduced in 1926 for mixed traffic working over various part of the LMS system, No. 13091 (later No. 2791) is near Hendon with an up Midland express, June 1928, in the maroon livery which these engines at first carried. Later in 1928 this was restricted to express passenger types.

Sir William Stanier also produced his own version of a 2-6-0 for mixed traffic purposes, again breaking away from LMS practice in the use of a taper boiler, a feature which he brought with him from Swindon; No. 13254 (later No. 2954) pauses in Penrith station, June 1935, with the Carlisle breakdown train.

One of the last new designs for the LMS before Nationalisation, introduced in 1946 by H. G. Ivatt, the company's last Chief Mechanical Engineer, and seen here at Wakefield in April 1949. There was also a corresponding 2-6-2T version. Both types continued to be built after Nationalisation, and were adopted as two of the twelve standard designs for further construction.

Another view of a Garratt, No. 4999 (later No. 7999) near Hendon in July 1928. Although these locomotives proved a useful stopgap in the absence of any larger eight-coupled engines, it was not until the appearance of Sir William Stanier's Class 8 2-8-0s in 1935 that the problem was really solved.

The Garratt design, patented by Bever Peacock, was never widely adopted in this country, although it has been, and still is, much used abroad. The only users to any extent were the L M S, who introduced 33 for the heavy freight trains between Toton and Cricklewood. They first appeared in 1927, intended as a means of avoiding the otherwise almost universal double-heading which was necessary, nothing larger than 0-6-0s being at that time available. 2-6+6-2 No. 4973 (later No. 7973), on a long rake of empty wagons, is passing Elstree, north-bound, in May 1931.

Meanwhile another attempt to avoid the continual double-heading necessary on the Midland was made in 1929, when Sir Henry Fowler Introduced a much-needed 0-8-0 engine for heavy freight use. Although of obvious Midland ancestry, that line had never had any eight-coupled engines in pre-Grouping days. No. 9561 is passing Elstree on a down train of empties, May 1931.

Two views of No. 8397, piloted by Class 4 No. 4185 passing Berkhamsted, March 1947. Stanier's 8F 2-8-0s of 1935 were quickly acclaimed and were soon to be seen on most of the LMS main lines south of the border. The design was adopted by the Government during the war and they were built in large numbers for use both at home and overseas.

Johnson 2-4-0 No. 127 with an up Bedford to St. Pancras train approaching Hendon, September 1927.

The first of the LMS compounds, No. 1000, running on to Derby shed in May 1934. This fine engine, a good deal changed in appearance since it was originally built by S. W. Johnson in 1902, is now preserved and restored to later MR condition. After running some enthusiasts' specials between 1959 and 1962, it was sent to Clapham Museum. Since closure in 1974, resulting in a move to York, No. 1000 is scheduled to take part in the 1975 Centenary procession, after which it will again be allowed to work occasional specials over the approved routes.

The 4-2-2 express single-wheeler of the late nineteenth century was almost extinct at the 1923 grouping. A few of Johnson's very fine design still remained, however, and one of the last survivors, No. 649, is seen in action near Hendon in September 1927 piloting compound No. 1015 on a down express. The last one of all to remain in traffic, No. 673, has fortunately been preserved.

For intermediate and some express trains, the LMS possessed a large number of these Class 2 4-4-0s, nominally Johnson engines rebuilt by Deeley, but in fact virtually new machines. The type was, with very slight modification, adopted as standard for new construction in the early years of the grouping. One of the original Midland engines, No. 557, heads an up express near Hendon, June 1928.

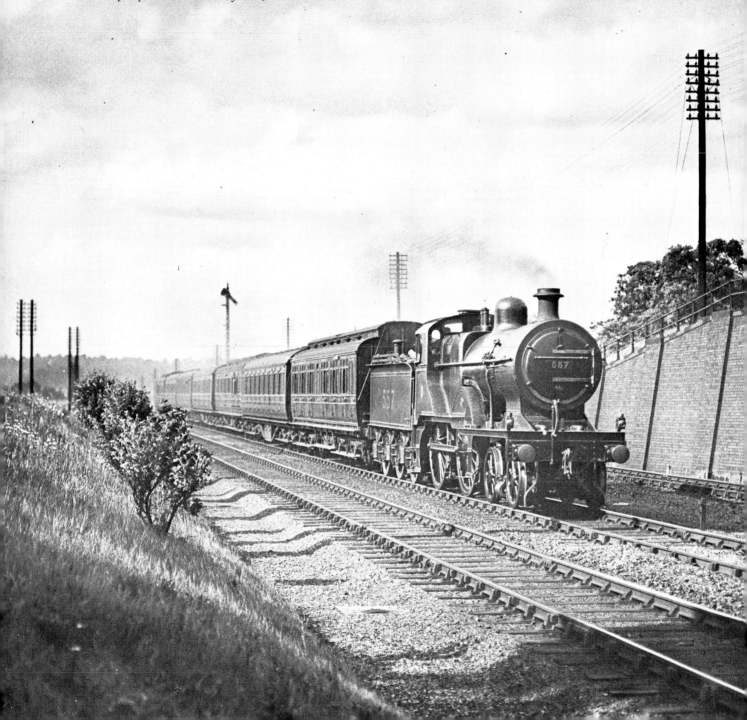

One of Johnson's last designs, the '700' Class, was introduced in 1900. Eighty of them were built, and together with the forty-five compounds, they were responsible for most of the main line expresses on the MR right up to the Grouping. That company never possessed anything larger than a 4-4-0 for its top link workings. No. 758, rebuilt with superheater and extended smokebox was, together with No. 759, loaned to the Midland & Great Northern Joint line in 1936 during the last few months of that railway's independent working before being taken over by the LNER in 1937. It is seen at South Lynn with a Yarmouth to Nottingham express, July 1936. M & GN drivers at the time maintained these were the best engines they had ever had.

**35**

Midland compound No. 1014 passing Longbridge Junction, near Birmingham,
May 1935, with a stopping train to Bristol.

The Midland compound was adopted as a standard design by the LMS for future construction, and a further 195 engines, additional to the original MR ones, were built. They did particularly well in Scotland as well as on the Birmingham two-hour expresses, although the LNWR in general never really took to them. No. 1183 is at the now-closed St. Enoch terminus in Glasgow waiting to depart with an express for Ayr, October 1946.

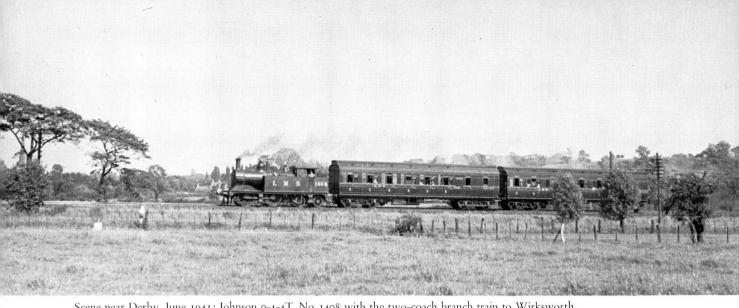

Scene near Derby, June 1941; Johnson 0-4-4T No. 1408 with the two-coach branch train to Wirksworth.

The station at Millers Dale on the picturesque Midland route between Derby and Manchester, the finest part of which, including this setting, is now entirely closed. This view, taken in June 1933, shows the branch train for Buxton into which passengers are changing from the main line express (on the left) to Manchester.

Another Johnson 0-4-4T, No. 1334, rebuilt with Belpaire firebox, working a local on the Somerset & Dorset line near Wincanton, July 1938.

A freight train ascending Shap, June 1935. The banking engine is a standard 'Jinty' 0-6-0T, No. 7663, a type directly descended from a Midland Johnson design and built in large numbers after the Grouping.

One of the original
Midland 0-6-0Ts,
No. 7253 (formerly
No. 1953), on station
pilot work at
Birmingham (New
Street), July 1935.

Another 'Jinty',
No. 16415 (later
No. 7332), on the
Highland Railway
branch train at Hopeman,
May 1928.

The famous Lickey incline banker, usually known as 'Big Bertha', was the Midland's largest engine, built in 1919 and the only one of its kind. For many years this was the only ten-coupled engine in this country apart from the short-lived 'decapod' of the GER in 1902. Originally No. 2290, it was renumbered 22290 in 1947 to make way for a new 2-6-4T. It is photographed at Bromsgrove in May 1948 preparatory to banking a train up the incline, over which it must have pounded its way well over a hundred thousand times during its 46 years of life. It was scrapped in 1956, but fortunately the unforgettable sound of the exhaust from its four cylinders has been preserved on a gramophone record.

Johnson Class 2F 0-6-0 No. 3195 on a Kettering to Cambridge train near Kimbolton, July 1939. This branch of the MR is now entirely closed.

One of Kirtley's double-framed 0-6-0s, No. 22852, dating back to 1873. Several hundred were built and many lasted into LMS days. This was one of the last few survivors which were retained for working the Halesowen branch, near Birmingham, owing to the light construction of Hunnington Viaduct and is seen near Rubery in May 1935, on a freight from the Austin motor works at Longbridge.

Up on the lonely heights of the Settle to Carlisle line, No. 3731 works a local pick-up goods at Garsdale (formerly Hawes Junction), not far from Ais Gill, the summit of the line. Moorcock Viaduct, one of the many on this route, can be seen in the background. Although there is no visual evidence of the fact, this photograph, taken in June 1935, was only secured with difficulty in driving rain.

Johnson Class 3 0-6-0 No. 3724 climbing the 1 in 37 Lickey incline, May 1935. Below, a war-time scene at Breadsall crossing, near Derby, June 1941, with 0-6-0 No. 3368 trundling over the level crossing with a local goods. The white painted wings of the author's car are a reminder of one of the precautions which had to be taken during the severe black-out restrictions of the time, nothing but severely dimmed side lights being allowed, and with complete absence of street lighting.

Fowler's Class 4 goods, first introduced in 1911, was another type selected by the LMS after the Grouping for future construction, which continued until 1940, by which time there were no less than 772 in service all over the system (including five originally built for the Somerset & Dorset). No. 4403 was photographed in August 1933 on a through freight between the LMS and SR over the West London Extension Railway at West Brompton.

Class 4 No. 4312 crossing Killiecrankie Viaduct on the Highland Railway, July 1931. Another view taken at this picturesque location appears as the frontispiece.

The North Stafford was one of the smaller lines which came into the LMS, although of considerable importance within its own area. Its locomotives included several classes of tank engines, including No. 2265, seen in May 1934 at the end of the rural branch to Waterhouses, from which ran the Leek & Manifold Valley Light Railway.

The busy London Tilbury & Southend Railway was originally an independent line, absorbed by the MR in 1912. Until the arrival of the Stanier 2-6-4Ts (see page 23) the passenger traffic was almost entirely in the hands of 4-4-2Ts, of which a typical example is seen in this view taken at Upminster in August 1926.

At the end of its independent existence, the LT & SR built eight large 4-6-4Ts, but they were never of much use to the line as their weight prohibited them from running into Fenchurch Street. As a consequence most of their careers were spent on the parent Midland system, either on suburban trains out of St. Pancras, as in this view taken at Elstree in May 1931, or on freight trains between Wellingborough and Cricklewood.

49

A former S & DJR engine, late No. 77, as LMS No. 320, at Bath in June 1930. This was one of a pair which, although with definite Midland characteristics (it was in fact built at Derby in 1908) was not quite like any engine to be found on the MR itself.

Sir Henry Fowler built eleven 2-8-0s for freight trains on the Somerset & Dorset Joint Railway's severe gradients, but rather surprisingly not for the parent Midland system, which never had anything larger than an 0-6-0 for goods working. One of them, No. 13808, at first numbered 9678 when the S & DJR engines were taken into LMS stock in 1930, is seen here near Wellow in September 1936. In more recent years the class was also often used on passenger work, especially during the busy holiday season, when there were a number of through trains, including the 'Pines Express', between the north of England and the south coast resorts of Poole and Bournemouth.

**5I**

Another former S & DJR engine at Highbridge in July 1930, recently renumbered and relettered, but retaining the Somerset & Dorset blue livery, as are the coaches, still carrying the initials of the S & DJR.

The LMS also acquired the Northern Counties Committee in Northern Ireland. Both under the MR and LMS regimes, most of the engines, which incidentally sported the fine crimson lake of the Midland, even the goods locomotives, usually carried just the initials NCC. This is one of the few which displayed on the tender the full LMS-NCC. No. 41, seen shunting at Londonderry resplendent in Midland red and with the brass beading around the splasher sparkling in the sunshine of an August day in 1930, would have been a fine subject for colour photography, but regrettably this did not exist in a practicable form in those days.

LNWR 2-4-2T No. 6674 at Peterborough East, May 1938, with a train over one of the now mainly closed cross-country lines to Rugby and Northampton.

One of the well-known LNWR 'Precedent' 2-4-0s, of which nearly a hundred came into LMS stock; No. 5005 *Pitt*, at Chester, September 1929.

No. 25319 *Bucephalus*, one of the last surviving 'Precursors', leaving Berkhamsted on a Northampton train, June 1939. The view is taken from the author's house.

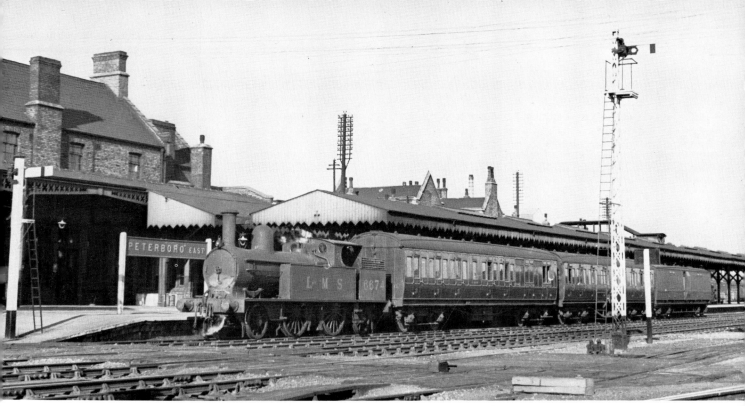

A double-ended LNWR pull-and-push train leaving Addison Road, Kensington, for Clapham Junction and East Croydon, over the West London Extension Railway, August 1933. The engine is Webb 4′ 10″ 0-6-2T No. 7710, dating back to 1884.

Superheated 'Precursor' No. 25188 *Marquis*, at Birmingham (New Street), July 1935. Most of these engines were superheated in later years, bringing them more into line with their successors, the 'George the Fifths'.

Cambridge was the most easterly outpost of the LMS system, both for the LNWR, which had its cross-country route from Bletchley and Bedford, and for the Midland, which once ran through trains from Kettering, although in this case over the lines of the GER from Huntingdon. LNWR 'Prince' No. 25722 is seen here at Cambridge in May 1938.

The last LNWR 'Claughton', No. 6004 (formerly *Princess Louise*), survived for several years after the rest of the class had disappeared, and was in fact not withdrawn until 1949. The illustration shows No. 6004 near Berkhamsted in May 1939 on the 6.06 p.m. from Euston, the main evening commuters' express to Northampton. This fine train (first stop Boxmoor), although suspended during the war years, was revived in 1946, and did not finally disappear until electrification in 1965.

Whale 'Precursor' tank No. 6784, with a stopping train at Penrith, a now closed station, on the LNWR main line south of Shap.

Verney Junction, on the LNWR Bletchley to Oxford line, now no longer served by passenger trains. The two-coach set, hauled by LNWR 'Cauliflower' 0-6-0 No. 8367, is signalled on to the Banbury branch, which diverged from the Oxford line here. This was also a junction making contact with the Metropolitan Railway, a rural outpost of that busy system, and the coaches seen on the right are part of a through train from Baker Street. This line is entirely abandoned.

An up goods train near Northchurch, May 1948, with one of the numerous LNWR 0-8-0s, No. 9127. This was the North Western's principal class for freight working up to the time of the Grouping, but in later years they were largely supplemented by Stanier 8F 2-8-0s.

Wembley Exhibition, 1925. All four of the groups shared a common railway stand in the Palace of Engineering, and each of them had a modern engine on display. The LMS exhibit comprised one of ten newly constructed large 4-6-4Ts of Lancashire & Yorkshire Railway design, although they did not actually appear until after the Grouping. They were in fact purely a tank version of the Hughes 4-6-0s, the L & Y's principal express type (see page 68).

The North London Railway, originally an independent concern, had very close associations with the LNWR, in fact since 1908 becoming virtually part of its system and being controlled by that company's Board of Directors. Otherwise it continued to operate as an independent concern until the time of the Grouping. NLR locomotive stock consisted mainly of a fleet of 4-4-0Ts for the unelectrified steam suburban services, which included through trains over the GNR to Potters Bar, Alexandra Palace and High Barnet. One of these engines, No. 6444, newly painted in LMS crimson lake, waits at Potters Bar in 1927.

For goods working, the NLR possessed a series of 0-6-0Ts. During the 1930s some of these were transferred far from their native haunts to surroundings as different as could be imagined, on the heights of the mineral line of the Cromford & High Peak Railway in Derbyshire. This included the steepest incline in the British Isles, 1 in 14, worked by ordinary adhesion without the use of cable haulage (of which the C&HPR also had two along its route). No. 7527 nears the summit of the incline in May 1934. Above, another illustration of an NLR 0-6-0T, No. 27530, on the Cromford & High Peak Railway, October 1940.

During the early part of the century, most railways experimented with steam railcars for branch line working as a means of economy on the operating costs of lightly loaded trains. These consisted of a combined engine and coach, usually in one complete unit with the engine enclosed in one end of the carriage, and of course with dual controls so that it could be driven in either direction without turning. The L & YR, however, had eighteen such units in which the engine was detachable and which could be exchanged with another coach should either be under repair. This is probably the reason why they lasted longer than those on other railways and, in fact, all passed into the hands of the LMS at the Grouping, one even surviving Nationalisation in 1948. Most had gone by the 1930s, however, one of the last survivors being No. 10616, seen here in Wakefield station, when it was at work on the Dearne Valley branch to Edlington.

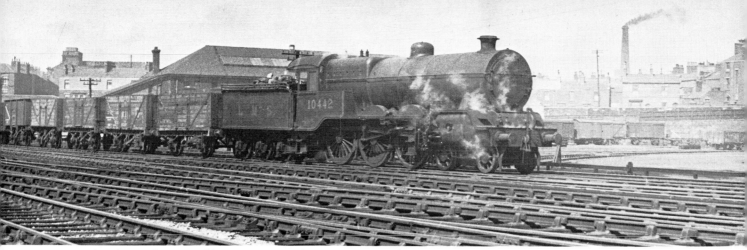

For their longer distance and heavier expresses, the L & YR possessed a stud of powerful 4-6-0s designed by George Hughes, the railway's last locomotive superintendent, who had been in office since 1904 and incidentally became for a couple of years the first CME of the LMS until replaced by Sir Henry Fowler of the MR in 1925. No. 10442 is seen on a freight train approaching Preston in April 1948.

The Lancashire & Yorkshire possessed a considerable number of 0-4-0 saddle tanks for working in its extensive dock areas. Two of these are seen at Bank Hall, Liverpool, in October 1946. Note the somewhat primitive form of spark arresters fitted to the chimneys.

Amongst the smaller lines acquired by the LMS was the Maryport & Carlisle. Most of its engines were very elderly and did not survive long under the new regime. It had, however, a couple of modern 0-6-0s, built in 1921, which lasted until 1934; one of these, No. 12513, is seen undergoing repair at Horwich works in July 1933.

The Furness Railway, serving the important industrial towns of Barrow, Whitehaven and Workington, together with much of Cumberland, was an important line in its area, and had about 140 engines at the time of the Grouping. 4-4-0 No. 10186 is seen here at Barrow Central station in July 1932. The overall roof has now been removed.

Away from the more industrial areas it served, the Furness also had branches to Coniston and into the Lake District, with its own steamers on the lakes at Coniston and Windermere. One of its 0-6-0s, No. 12501, stands at Coniston in picturesque surroundings, June 1935.

North of the border, the Caledonian was the largest of the three Scottish railways to come into the orbit of the LMS. One of its best known engines was the solitary single-wheeler, No. 123, built by Neilsen & Co in 1886, and exhibited at the Edinburgh Exhibition in that year. This engine took part in the 1888 race to Scotland and in later years was put to work hauling the directors' saloon. In 1930, however, it was returned to ordinary service to run light trains over the virtually level line between Perth and Dundee and is seen on this service leaving Dundee in May 1930, then in LMS crimson lake livery and with the new number 14010. By this time it was the last express single-wheeler in use in the British Isles. The more recent history of this locomotive is fairly well known. Withdrawn in 1935 and put in store for preservation, it was restored to working order in 1958 in original CR blue livery and for several years was seen on enthusiasts' specials all over the country, even as far south as Sussex. It now has a permanent resting place in Glasgow museum.

72

An old Caledonian goods engine of 1881, 0-4-2 No. 17018, at Dundee in May 1930 shortly before withdrawal.

Pickersgill 4-6-0 No. 14620 approaching Oban in June 1927. One of the most picturesque routes of the old CR was the Callander and Oban line, running through the mountainous scenery of Argyll to the west coast.

Amongst the best remembered of all CR engines were the 'Cardean' Class 4-6-0s introduced by J. F. McIntosh in 1903. This is the first of the class, No. 49, as LMS No. 14750, at Perth in May 1930, after working an express from Aberdeen.

The formidable Beattock bank, on the main line between Carlisle and Glasgow, consisting of ten miles of continuous ascent of gradients varying between 1 in 74 and 1 in 88, always required the services of a banking engine in steam days. A favourite type for this duty were the McIntosh 0-4-4Ts, four of which were specially fitted with strengthened cast-iron front buffer beams for this duty. One of them, No. 15238, commences the climb with an eleven-coach express at the head of which is compound No. 901, August 1931.

A short branch off the Callander and Oban main line at Killin Junction ran down to the small holiday resort of Killin, and to Loch Tay. The branch train is seen here in July 1931, in charge of 0-4-4T, No. 15103. It was completely closed in 1965.

Of all the locomotives acquired by the LMS at the Grouping, those of the Glasgow & South Western, along with the North Stafford, fared the worst. Indeed, on the latter railway all had been taken out of service by 1939, and the position on the G&SWR was not much better, for most had been scrapped by that time, although a few did survive the war. This typical elderly Manson 0-6-0 of 1892 vintage was still to be seen at Corkerhill in May 1928.

Stranraer Harbour, August 1930, with a double-headed boat train about to leave for Glasgow. The nearest engine is a G & S W R Manson 4-4-0, of 1896, which was destined to be scrapped in the following year, whilst the pilot is a Caledonian Dunalastair III, No. 14340, of 1900; this too only survived until 1939.

G & S W R 4-4-0 No. 14135, built by H. Smellie in 1885, at now closed St. Enoch station in Glasgow, August 1930. At that period this station was alive with these 4-4-0s, of varying classes, but they were very soon to be replaced by LMS standard Class 2s such as No. 578, seen in the background.

Amongst the few G & S W R engines to survive the war period were several of the Whitelegg 0-6-2Ts, which first came out in 1919. No. 16907 had been transferred to the Highland section for banking up to Druichmuchdar summit, and waits at Blair Atholl in June 1937, ready for this duty. One of the class survived into the Nationalisation period, but was withdrawn early in 1948.

One of the larger-wheeled versions of the same basic 'Skye bogie' design, intended in the first place for express working over the main lines, No. 14276 *Glenbruar*. Built in 1892, it is seen entering Alves Junction, in May 1928, on a local from Elgin to Inverness.

The Highland was, in many ways, the most interesting and fascinating of all the components of the LMS, both on account of its scenery, which is unlike anything else to be found in the British Isles, at any rate outside Scotland, but also the unique character of its locomotives. Perhaps most important of this aspect was the period from 1869 to 1896 when David Jones was locomotive superintendent. A typical design of his was the 'Skye bogie', produced especially for the severe curves and abounding gradients of the beautiful Kyle of Lochalsh line. No. 14279 is seen here at the Kyle of Lochalsh, gateway to the island of Skye, in June 1937. This line is still open, although it has on more than one occasion been threatened with closure during and since the Beeching era.

David Jones' last design for the Highland was his splendid 'Loch' Class, introduced in 1896, of which fifteen appeared during that year. So successful were these that when more locomotives were required in 1917 during urgent war conditions, three more were built, reliance being placed on an old and well tried design rather than something new. No. 14396, *Loch Ruthven*, was the last of these three, and is seen here under busy and animated conditions at Inverness in May 1928.

A rather smaller engine, No. 14278, built in 1886, running round its train at Fochabers, May 1928. Elderly express engines were often used by the Highland to work out their time on branch line duties. No. 14278 was the only one of the class to survive the Grouping.

Most of the 'Lochs' were rebuilt in later years with larger boilers, including No. 14379 *Loch Insh*, here leaving Aviemore in June 1927 piloting No. 14766 *Clan Chattan* on a south-bound express.

One of the 'Ben' Class 4-4-0s introduced by Peter Drummond in 1898, No. 14398 *Ben Alder*, seen running round its train at the terminus of the short Strathpeffer branch in May 1928. Note the Sentinel railcar in the background (see page 96).

Britain's most northerly engine shed, Thurso, May 1928. No. 14405 *Ben Rinnes* is on the turntable between duties of working the through coaches from the south between Thurso and Georgemas Junction, where these were detached from or attached to the main train between Inverness and Wick. Nearly all Highland express engines were named, and it was pleasant that these were retained after the Grouping when being repainted at Lochgorm works, Inverness, as by contrast the few Caledonian engines which had borne names had them removed when they passed through the CR works at St. Rollox. The first few years of the Grouping could perhaps

be described as the golden age of the Highland. After the somewhat drab green, the engines looked really magnificent in the fine MR crimson lake, and were kept in beautiful condition. Subsequent to 1928, when black was declared the official livery for all but the top link express engines, no locomotives working on the HR qualified. It could be said that this was the period the general decline set in; engines were no longer so well cared for, which led gradually to the later years, especially during and after the war, when cleaning became a thing of the past and resulted in the shabby appearance of most locomotives during the final years of steam.

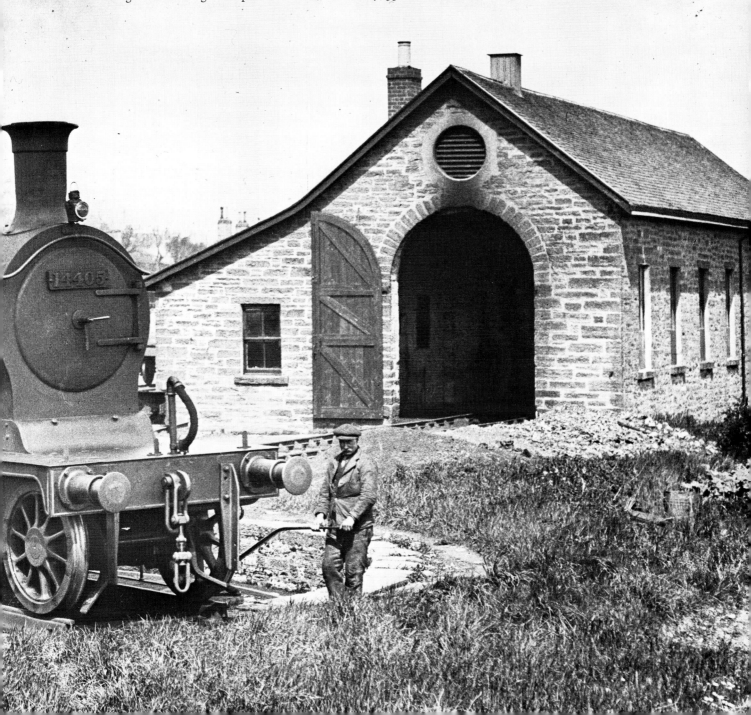

Another very successful class, Drummond's 'Castles', introduced in 1900, were to be the mainstay of the HR express working for very many years, at any rate until the appearance of the 'Clans' in 1921, and even then they were only displaced to a limited extent. No. 14677 *Dunrobin Castle* is seen here at Aviemore in July 1931, piloting No. 14761, a type originally built for the HR in 1915 but found too heavy for the line and transferred to the Caledonian. Only after the Grouping was it found possible to transfer these to the railway for which they had been intended, but they were never very satisfactory and all but one disappeared before the war.

A larger version of the 'Small Bens' (see pages 87 and 88) were the 'Big Bens', six of which came out in 1908–09; No. 14418 *Ben Mheadhoin*, with an old HR six-wheeler, in rainy conditions at Aviemore in May 1928.

No. 15010, one of three 4-4-0Ts built by David Smith for branch line work in 1878-79, seen at Inverness in May 1930. The striking similarity with the North London 4-4-0Ts will be noted by comparison with the illustration on page 64.

David Jones is perhaps best remembered by his introduction of the 4-6-0 type to Great Britain. The first of these, No. 103, appeared in 1894, and is fortunately now preserved in Glasgow museum. No. 17919 is seen here on a stopping train entering Killiecrankie station in July 1931.

The Highland's final express engines were built by its last locomotive superintendent, Christopher Cummings, in 1919 and 1921. No. 14767 *Clan Mackinnon*, again resplendent in LMS crimson lake livery and in beautiful condition, amid the pleasant setting of Inverness shed in May 1928.

One of the few narrow gauge passenger lines to be inherited by the LMS was the Leek & Manifold Valley Light Railway, a subsidiary of the North Stafford. Opened in 1904, its nine miles ran through the beautiful valley of the rivers Manifold and Hamps, from the small township of Waterhouses, terminus of a standard gauge NSR branch' to Hulme End, which was literally in the middle of nowhere, being over two miles from the villages of Sheen and Hartington it was supposed to serve. Even the other hamlets *en route* were a mile or two distant from the stations. The gauge was 2ft. 6in. The chief traffic was in milk, the passenger element being of a tourist nature, and naturally seasonal. Small wonder that it closed in 1934 after a life of only thirty years. The trackbed was purchased by the Staffordshire County Council and converted to a paved footpath. The two views show respectively a train near Sparrowlee and at the terminus at Hulme End, the engine in both cases being No. 2
*J. B. Earle*, June 1933.

Following the example of the LNER, which in 1925 introduced Sentinel steam railcars for branch line working, the LMSR introduced a series of somewhat similar vehicles. These made use of high speed gear-drive transmission in place of the conventional cylinders and direct drive of an orthodox steam locomotive, together with the employment of a high-pressure vertical boiler. Fourteen were produced between 1925 and 1928, and these worked on various parts of the system until the end of the 1930s. One of them is seen here working on the Strathpeffer branch of the Highland in May 1928.